DOG

The Complete Guide on Raising

Dog Training Basics and Positive Reinforcements

By Rex Jackson

TABLE OF CONTENTS

INTRODUCTION

Dog training is applying behavioral analysis that uses the context and effects of environmental events to change the dog's actions, either to assist in specific activities or to perform specific tasks or to engage effectively in contemporary domestic life. Although training dogs for particular roles dates back to the Roman era, in the 1950s, dogs' training to be compatible household pets grew with suburbanization.

A dog learns from its experiences with its surroundings. This can be by classical conditioning. Two stimuli form an association; non-associative learning, in which its behavior is changed by habit or sensitization; and operative conditioning, in which an antecedent and its effect are linked.

There are several known methods of training animals, each with its supporters and critics. The Koehler process, clicker training, motivational training, computer training, model-rival training, dominance-based training, and relationship-based training are some of the better-known dog training procedures. Knowing the animal's attributes and personality, the precise timing of reward or punishment, and consistent communication are the common characteristics of successful approaches. With both the humaneness and efficacy of many behaviorists, the use of punishment is contentious.

CHAPTER 1

HOUSETRAINING YOUR DOG

House-training requires patience, determination, and plenty of consistency with your dog or puppy. Accidents are part of the process, but in a few weeks, you can get the newest member of your family on the right track if you follow these simple housetraining guidelines.

Establish a Routine

Puppies do well on a daily schedule, much like kids. The schedule tells them that there are times for sleeping, playing time, and times for doing their business. Generally speaking, with each month of age, a puppy will regulate its bladder for one hour. So if your dog is two months old, they'll be able to keep it for two hours or so. Between bathroom breaks, don't go longer than that, or they're guaranteed to have an accident.

Take your puppy outside regularly and soon after they wake up, during and after playing, and after eating or drinking, at least every two hours.

Outside, choose a bathroom spot, and always take your puppy to that spot (on a leash). Use a particular word or expression that you will finally use before reminding them what to do when your puppy is relieving itself. Only after they have been removed take them out for a longer walk or some playtime.

Reward your puppy every time they go outside. But remember to do so right after they've done, not after they come back inside. Praise or offer treats. This move is important, as the best way to teach what is expected of them is to reward your dog for going outside. Before you reward them, be sure they're done. Puppies are easily distracted, and they can forget to finish before they're back in the house if you praise them too soon.

Put your puppy on a schedule for daily feeding. On a schedule, what goes into a puppy comes out of a puppy. Puppies normally need to be fed three or four times a day, depending on their size. Feeding your puppy at the same times per day will make it more likely that they will also remove them at regular times, making it easier for both of you to do home training.

To decrease the chance that they will need to relieve

themselves during the night, pick up your puppy's water dish around two and a half hours before bedtime. Without having a bathroom break, most puppies will sleep for approximately seven hours. Do not make a big deal of it if your dog wakes you up in the night; otherwise, they will think it's time to play, and they won't want to go back to sleep. Turn on as few lights as possible, don't talk to your dog or play with him, take them out, and then bring them back in bed.

Monitor Your Puppy

Don't give a puppy a chance to land in the house; keep an eye on them while they're indoors.

When you are not actively training or playing, tie your puppy to you or a nearby piece of furniture with a six-foot leash. Watch for indications that you need your puppy to go out. Some symptoms are evident, such as barking at the door or scratching, squatting, restlessness, sniffing, or circling about. Grab the leash immediately when you see these signs and drive them outside to their place in the bathroom. If they do, compliment them and reward them with a treat.

Hold your dog in the yard on a leash. Your yard should be handled like every other space in your home during the housetraining process. Only after they become consistently housetrained give your puppy some freedom in the house and yard.

USING A CRATE TO HOUSE TRAIN PUPPY

A crate can be a good idea, at least in the short term, for home training your puppy. It will encourage you to keep an eye on them for signals that they need to go and teach them to hold it until the crate is opened and left out.

Here are a few tips on how to use a crate:

- Ensure that the puppy is wide enough to stand, turn around and lie down, but not big enough to use a corner as a toilet for them.

- Make sure the puppy has fresh water if you are using the box for more than two hours at a time, preferably in a dispenser you can connect to the box.

- If you can't be home during house training, make

sure someone else gives them a break for the first eight months in the middle of the day.

- If your dog gets out of it, do not use a crate. There may be several meanings to eliminate in the crate: they may have brought bad habits from the shelter or pet store where they once lived; they may not get out enough; the crate may be too big, or they may be too young to keep it in.

Signs That Your Puppy Needs to Eliminate

Whining, circling, sniffing, barking, or barking or scratching at the door, if your dog is unconfined, are all signs they need to go. Right now, take them out.

Setbacks in House Preparation

For puppies up to a year old, accidents are normal. The causes for injuries vary from incomplete house training to a change in the climate of the puppy.

Keep on working when your dog has an accident. Visit a veterinarian to rule out a medical condition if it still doesn't seem to be working.

Do's and Don'ts of Your Puppy's Potty Training

Keep the do's and don'ts in mind during your puppy's home training:

It is a definite no-no to punish your dog for having an accident. Your puppy is trained to fear you.

If you catch your puppy in the act, clap loudly, so they know something unacceptable has been done. Then take them by calling them outside or softly taking them by the neck. Praise them when they are done, or give them a little treat.

If you find the evidence but did not see the act, do not respond angrily by shouting or rubbing your nose in it. Intellectually, puppies aren't capable of relating your rage to their accident.

Staying outside with your puppy longer can help curb accidents. They can need to explore the extra time.

To eliminate odors that might draw the puppy back to the same place, clean up incidents with an enzymatic cleanser rather than an ammonia-based cleaner.

BASIC OBEDIENCE TRAINING FOR DOGS

A crucial aspect of becoming a conscientious dog owner is learning simple obedience commands. These simple orders make it much easier to manage the relationship between the animal and the owner and keep you and your pet safe in emergencies.

Basic training can look either very easy or incredibly complex from the viewpoint of an outsider. Recognize that it can take a lot of work to train. Recognize that any dog should at least learn the most basic and essential instructions. When exercising, dog owners often run into roadblocks and do not get upset. First-time owners or people are struggling with teaching commands or correcting troublesome habits profit from finding assistance from a trainer. Do not ever hesitate to ask for assistance!

Even if you aren't doing any complex or 'fancy' tricks, preparation requires a lot of time and patience. The task of pet ownership requires properly educating and socializing your pet. Please consider how much time you will need to devote to making sure you have a happy, safe, well-socialized, and well-trained animal before considering adopting an animal.

Finally, it should be enjoyable for dog ownership and even training! Don't be too serious, and make sure you and your pet have a nice time so that you can look forward to future meetings!

STEP 1

What Do You Need

1. A dog!

2. A place in which to learn while you are first training your dog, where it is free from distractions. You'll want to switch to places with more distractions, such as outside, as you and your dog master commands, to continue enhancing your dog's willingness to concentrate on you and the commands.

3. Treats or a toy as prizes. Find out what works for both your dog and you. Some dogs are very food-driven, and as their reward, some dogs enjoy toys and play. Furthermore, remember the size of the treats that you use during preparation! Treats that are too big easily fill up a dog, so look for tiny training treats.

4. For distance practice, a short leash, and a longer training leash.

5. Expectations that are rational!

For the first few tries, don't plan to get it done. It takes a lot of time to teach and master certain commands.

Try to make training sessions at most about 15 minutes long.

There will be moments where you and your dog are both upset. Only switch on to another or better-established command when struggling with a certain command. Come back to the one in which you are struggling later.

End training on a good note ALWAYS. Both you and your pet, this makes the training sessions enjoyable. Next time, when it is time to train, your dog will be excited!

STEP 2

Sit Command

1. Make sure you've got the attention of your dog and a treat in hand. Stand or kneel before your dog and hold your hand slightly higher than the head of your dog.

2. By slowly pushing the reward straight back over the dog's head and towards the tail, use the treat to direct the

dog into position. Your dog should point up his nose and drop towards the ground with his rear.

3. When the dog moved securely into the sitting position, say 'Sit' and make the hand gesture shown in Image 2.

4. Your dog is rewarded with a treat and some encouragement as soon as the dog moves into place, such as saying, 'Nice sit! '

5. You can help direct them with a gentle push if your dog has trouble understanding. Place two fingers on his hips and drive his rear gently towards the ground while saying 'Sit' firmly.

STEP 3

Down Command

Your dog should already know the Sit Command for this trick. It can be a little harder to learn this command because it is a very submissive pose for your dog to take.

1. Kneel in front of your dog, with your dog in a sitting place.

2. Keep a treat in front of your dog's nose and direct it

by slowly lowering the threat to the carpet.

3. Your dog can just slouch as he heads downwards. If this occurs, to further direct him, move the treatment towards or away from your dog appropriately.

4. Reward him with a reward and encouragement as soon as your dog is in the right place.

5. If you have trouble directing your dog into the Down position, you can direct him physically by putting a hand on the shoulders of your dog and pushing it down to the side softly while the command is being spoken. As soon as he drops to the floor, thank your dog.

STEP 4

Stay Command

Your dog should also be able to perform either the sitting or lying positions to master this order. To support the preparation, you will need both a short lead (6 ') and a longer lead.

1. Start in a sitting or down position with your dog.

2. Standing in front of your dog, say 'Wait' firmly while making the hand signal.

3. Although maintaining eye contact with your dog, travel a short distance away.

4. If your dog stays in place, then step back toward him and reward him while still sitting with a treat and praise. You should move to a longer lead and distance as the response of your dog improves. In a fenced area, you will finally begin practicing off-leash.

5. Guide your dog back to the sitting position in the original location if your dog breaks position, and try again.

STEP 5

Come Command

Your dog should already know the 'Down' or 'Down' and 'Wait' instructions to start working on this command. For this command, you will need a longer lead.

1. Walk a few distances away from the dog on a long lead with the dog in the Sit or Lay and Stay position.

2. Tell 'Come' strongly, but politely, and make the hand gesture seen in Picture 2. When required, then reel your dog in with the rope. Just once should you say this order!

14

3. Reward him with a treat and encouragement as soon as your dog hits him.

4. If your dog progresses, you will be able to start off-leash practice in a fenced area. If your dog refuses to come off-leash, then return to using the long lead before he starts responding to the coming command correctly and reliably.

CHAPTER 2
POTTY TRAIN A PUPPY

Introduce your new pup to their new home, their position, and their family. Your new pet may be bursting with curiosity, enthusiasm, fear, or joy, just like when you are new to a location or community. Now is the perfect time to lay out your pet's groundwork to have a healthy and friendly relationship. It is very important to define your puppy's expectations and be consistent with them for a puppy to settle in and learn to trust and appreciate you and everyone at home.

Show your pet just the places where it is supposed to be. Do not initially allow your new pet to wander and explore on its own, particularly if you do not want them to do their business there. For instance, close them off if the upstairs area or bedrooms are off-limits and do not encourage your puppy to explore there.

Understand the complex racial behavior and needs of your puppy. Study your dogs' attributes and special needs or any actions you should be aware of and watch out for.

If your puppy is a small little chihuahua, for example, their bladder will be very tiny, and they will need to urinate more often; accidents will occur even if they are well trained.

Although most dogs are highly intelligent, they don't think like people do. When we ask them to comprehend basic command words or tell you that they need to pee or poop, it is always an issue. You must learn how they deal with you and research the hints they offer and get from you for this purpose.

Your dog, keep an eye on it. When potty training, having your puppy where you can watch it at all times is best. This will encourage you to look for early signals that you need to go to help avoid accidents when they start to circle, scratch, and sniff.

Whining, circling, sniffing, barking, or some abrupt shift of conduct are some of the signs to watch for. When you see any of these signals, lead the dog outside immediately.

Interrupting crashes. In the act of urinating or defecating indoors, if you catch your puppy, make a sudden noise like a clap and say the word "no." Then lead the dog outside quickly.

You want to startle the puppy, but not to frighten it. The intention here is to get their immediate attention and to know that you disagree with indoor marking or pooping. You want to be consistent as well, each time using the same word and/or noise.

If the dog is defecating, you will not get the same outcome because most puppies will not avoid this. Yet, as part of the teaching process, you can always do the same thing.

Never punish your dog because of an accident. The dog doesn't know that something bad is being done. Do not push your dog to smell their actions or keep reminding them of them. They may not remember you and will become afraid of you.

This will confuse your dog and even make things worse if you use discipline to stop them from going indoors. Your dog will only understand that when you see them potty, you get angry and will hide from you when they need to go, most likely in areas that are difficult for you to reach.

Select a zone for a potty. Any time it needs to go, it is best to find a certain place outside and drive your dog there. You should choose a location that other dogs do not frequent and that is easy to clean up.

Your puppy will recognize the urine scent and begin to associate the area with his "bathroom."

Select an area that is easy to quickly get to. During the training process, you can visit this area regularly.

You should avoid places where other dogs are going or have recently gone, such as parks, until your puppy has had its third set of vaccinations. Discussing this with your veterinarian is a good idea.

It is a good idea to keep your dog on a leash when you take it outside, so you can train it to go to a specific spot. You can also keep an eye on the dog more easily, so you will know when it's done.

Choose a particular command of a sound or phrase. Use the word "go," or choose another command each time you take your puppy outside their neighborhood. This will teach him to go to that particular place.

The dog will start to learn and understand the order and what you want to do. This will help the dog understand when it should be urinating or defecating and where it should be.

Just use the command when you want them to go. This will prevent ambiguity

Achievements of Appreciation

Any time it uses the right place, always praise your puppy. Using a joyful, cheerful voice that lets the dog know you are pleased with it.

Being consistent with this would give them an emotional motivation to be in the right position to do their business.

For your dog, make the potty time a calming and enjoyable experience to look forward to. They must first enjoy it to motivate your dog to hang on patiently and wait before you allow them to go.

It should be a satisfying experience for any dog to enjoy going out for a walk and relieving themselves.

If they are doing their business where you want them to go, do not bother your dog. Enable them to relax, relieve themselves, and loosen up.

Afterward, you can also give a small reward to your puppy to help inspire it. This can also be a diversion for certain dogs, though.

Clean up injuries immediately. When your dog has an indoor accident, it is necessary to thoroughly clean the area. This will hopefully deter the dog from having to go to the same location again.

Using an enzymatic cleaner, not an ammonia-containing one. This will help to eliminate the smell and the attraction of the dog to the place.

Urine has a strong ammonia scent that draws dogs to smell and identify themselves. For the latter, certain training pads to enable a puppy to go there are sprayed with ammonia.

To counteract the odor of ammonia, you may also use white vinegar.

STEPS TO TAKE WHIL TRAINING YOUR DOG

Keeping Your Dog Close

1. Limit the space around the dog. Keeping a close eye on your puppy would be simpler if you limit the dog to a certain region of your house. You can do this by closing doors and using baby gates.

If your dog is restricted to a smaller location, to decide if it wants to go outside, you will be able to observe it continuously.

For the puppy to play in, the field should be big enough but tiny enough that you can see it at all times. A small space is preferable or a sectioned off part of a room.

Be sure to select an area with simple, easy access to the outdoors. Space is best with a door leading straight outside.

It's also a smart idea to choose an area which is easy to clean. In the early stages of preparation, there would be injuries.

2. Keep the puppy on a short leash. Keeping the dog on a leash helps you to move more easily while keeping a close eye on your puppy, even while indoors.

You can switch from room to room with your dog on a leash and keep your puppy with you. That way, there is never going to be a moment when you can't see it.

Getting the dog already on a leash often ensures that, if necessary, you can take it outside more easily.

3. When you can't look at the puppy, use a crate. Using a crate can be a successful way to help potty train when you leave home or can not watch your puppy. Your puppy will learn to see the crate as its "home" and be reluctant to soil their field.

For the dog to stand up, lay down, and turn around, the crate should be just big enough. The dog can use one area as a bathroom and another area to sleep if the crate is too big.

Limit the amount of time the dog spends in the crate at any one time to less than four hours.

Establishing a Routine

1. Be cohesive. One of the keys to potty training is to be consistent. It is safer to still use the same door when taking your puppy outside. You should still take the dog to the same spot and use the same command to associate the suitable action with the location.

Establish a routine to take the dog out. In the morning

and after every meal, do it first thing. Whenever you come home or take them out of the cage, take your dog outside. After playing or drinking water, after napping, and just before bedtime, let your puppy out.

You should also consider getting the dog out every 20 minutes or so, where possible, with very young puppies and in the early stages of training. This will help prevent injuries and give you more reasons to thank your dog for getting to the right spot.

To motivate the dog to go, daily walks can also help.

2 Learn how long it takes your dog to go. Pay careful attention to how much urinating is important for your puppy. This will help you understand their routine and anticipate when a trip outside needs to be made.

3 Around mealtimes, plan trips outside. It can help with a daily potty schedule to maintain a regular feeding schedule. Puppies usually need to go immediately after eating.

After every meal, getting your dog out will reinforce the definition of where they are supposed to go while minimizing the mess.

CHAPTER 3
HOW TO GET YOUR PUP
TO LISTEN TO YOU

I t can be frustrating when your dog does not listen to your instructions, and it can also be risky. This form of contact will, after all, help keep your dog out of trouble, stop him from running into a busy street, or eating anything he shouldn't. By helping you handle problem habits, it will also help keep you sane.

But getting to the root of the problem is not always easy. So, where do you begin if your dog doesn't obey, either in particular circumstances or all the time? Here are a few issues you may experience.

Remove Excess Energy

If you've ever tried to engage with a hyper toddler, then you know how it can distract excited energy. For dogs, it's no different. His only emphasis is on releasing all that pent-up energy inside while your pup is raring to go, and he's going to have a tough time listening to you.

So remember to practice exercise first, then discipline, love. A daily walk that genuinely drains all the energy from your dog can go a long way.

Be Consistent

He won't understand what you want from him if your dog gets different signals about his actions. That's also valid if individual family members follow various laws. Sit down as a family and address the rules you want to set for your dog, limits, and restrictions. Writing them down and showing them somewhere prominently can be helpful.

Master Your Energy

Dogs listen to their pack leaders, and only if you show calm-assertive energy can you be that leader. Your dog will tune you out if you are frantic or uncertain when you offer an order. Sadly, a lot of people are not mindful of the energy that we're giving away. Have a friend watch and give you feedback on your actions, or even film it to see yourself.

Go Back to Basics

Is your dog very familiar with that command? For

certain dogs to learn a new ability, it can take hundreds or even thousands of repetitions. Work renders fine. To ensure your dog has it down, you will need to work on training again.

Stopping depending on verbal orders

Dogs don't talk to one another; to communicate, they use energy and body language. So it's not surprising that sometimes they have trouble picking up on our verbal orders, especially when our relentless yammering all day bombards them.

They might simply connect it more with a non-verbal signal you send simultaneously, even though they know an order, something you may not even realize you're doing.

Consider what could have changed about your physical appearance if your dog listens to you. Keeping a baby, are you? Sitting back, are you? Will you look away? Small changes such as these can affect your ability to fully communicate your message as you would normally do.

Notice Your Dog's Emotional State

Your dog may be overwhelmed by a variety of emotions beyond pent-up energy. Instead, your pup might be so focused on claiming her turf that she's tuned you out if you are trying to teach her to come when a neighbor's dog approaches. Or maybe she's so terrified of the sound of thunder and lightning that there's little room in her mind to hear your command to go to her box. Before you can get your dog to truly listen to you, you have to deal with the root issue.

Try hiring a specialist to help if you continue to have issues. For both of you, contact between you and your dog is important and worth your time and energy commitment.

5 BASIC COMMANDS FOR DOGS

To teach your dog, are you looking for the best commands? Although having a trained dog is not the same as having a healthy dog, teaching simple dog training instructions to your dog may help solve behavioral issues regardless of whether they are current ones or those that might evolve in the future.

And where exactly do you begin to teach commands

to your dog? Although taking a class can help you and your pet, you can teach your dog right at home with several dog training commands. We have mentioned below the best list of dog orders that you and your puppy are sure to enjoy.

Sit, sit

One of the most basic dog commands to teach your pet is to teach your dog to sit, thereby making it a perfect one, to begin with. "It would be much calmer and easier to handle a dog who knows the "Sit" command than dogs who are not taught this basic command. Also, the "Sit" command prepares your dog for more challenging commands like "Stay" and "Come."

Here is how to teach the command "Sit" to your dog:

- Keeping a treat close to the nose of your dog.

- Step your hand up, allowing the treat to be accompanied by his head and causing his bottom to drop.

- Tell "Sit," give him the treat once he is in a sitting position, and express love.

- Repeat this sequence until your dog has learned it a few times per day. Then ask your dog to sit before mealtime, when you go for walks, and when you want him relaxed and seated during other scenarios.

- Come, come and come

The word 'come' is another vital command for your dog to understand. For those occasions when you lose hold of the leash or unintentionally leave the front door open, this command is incredibly helpful. This order, again, is simple to teach and will help keep your dog out of trouble.

- Place your dog on a leash and a collar.

- Go down to his level and say "Come" while pulling on the leash gently.

- Reward him with love and a treat when he gets to you.

- Remove it and continue to practice the command in a secure, enclosed environment until he has mastered it with the leash.

Down

One of the most challenging dog training commands to teach is this next instruction. The explanation that learning this command can be difficult for your dog is that it allows him to be in a submissive pose. By maintaining positive and comfortable training, especially if your dog is fearful or anxious, you can help your dog out. Bear in mind, too, to always compliment your dog until he follows the order successfully.

- Find and keep an especially nice smelling treat in your closed fist.

- Keep your hand up towards the snout of your dog. Shift your hand to the floor when he sniffs it, so he follows.

- Then move your hand in front of him along the ground to allow his body to follow his brain.

- Say "Down" while he's in the down role, give him the medication, and share the love.

- Repeat each day of this preparation. Tell "No" and pull your hand away if your dog wants to sit or lunge at your hand. Don't pressure him into a down position, and allow your dog to take every move in the correct position. He's working hard to find it out, after all!

- Stay

The "Stay" signal will help make your dog easier to manage, similar to the "Sit" order. In various cases, including those occasions when you want your dog out of the way as you tend to household tasks or when you don't want your pup overwhelming visitors, this order may be beneficial.

Make sure your dog is an expert at the "Sit" cue before attempting to teach your dog this order. If he has not yet mastered the "Sit" order, before moving on to the "Stay" cue, take the time to practice it with him.

- Next, ask the dog to "sit down."

- Then open the hand palm in front of you and say, "Stay."

- Take several steps back. Reward him if he lives, with a treat and love.

- Until giving the care, progressively increase the

number of steps you take.

- Always praise your dog, even if it's only for a few seconds, for staying put.

This is a self-control exercise for your dog, so if it takes a while to learn, particularly for puppies and high-energy dogs, don't be discouraged. Many dogs, after all, rather than just sitting and waiting, tend to be on the move.

Leave it

When his curiosity gets the best of him, such as those times when he smells something interesting but potentially dangerous on the field, this last command will help keep your dog safe. The goal is to teach your pup that he gets something even better if he ignores the other object.

- Insert a treat in both hands.

- "Show him one closed fist inside with the treat and say, "Drop it.

- To get the treat, ignore the behavior as he licks, sniffs, noses, paws, and barks.

- Offer him the treat from the other side until he finishes trying.

- Repeat until if you say "Leave it," your dog moves away from the first fist.

- Next, just offer the treat to your dog if he looks up at you as he steps away from the first fist.

You're able to step it up a notch until your dog slowly moves away from the first reward and gives you eye contact when you say the order. Use two separate therapies for this next training method: one that is decent but not super-appealing and one that is especially good for your dog and delicious.

- Say "Leave it," put on the floor the less-attractive treat and cover it with your hand.

- Wait for your dog to forget the treatment and smile at you. Then take the treat from the floor, give him the best treatment, and instantly exchange love.

- Place the less-tasty treat on the floor until he's got it, but do not cover it with your hand. Hold your hand a little bit above the treat, instead. Slowly shift your hand further and further away over time until your hand is about 6 inches higher.

- He's happy now to practice standing up with you! Take the same steps, but cover it with your foot if he attempts to grab the less-tasty treat.

- Do not rush the process of teaching any of these dog training commands to your pup. Remember, you ask your dog a lot. Go back to the previous stage if you step things up a notch and he's still struggling.

This list of dog instructions will help secure and enhance your dog's communication from dangerous circumstances. The commitment of your time and effort is well worth taking the time to teach your pup these traditional dog commands. Know, the training process takes time, so only if you are in the correct mindset to practice calm-assertive energy and patience, start a dog obedience training session.

CHAPTER 4

WHY PUP USES THE BATHROOM INSIDE AFTER YOU JUST TOOK HIM OUT

D ogs that are completely housetrained can suddenly start soiling in the house due to stress and anxiety due to medical conditions or. Test if you have recently relocated, changed schedules, or are keeping your dog at home for a longer period than he is used to if medical problems are ruled out.

When they feel frightened or stressed out, dogs poop and pee from lack of balance, this activity can be reduced by recognizing and eliminating environmental stressors.

1. Overstimulation During Potty Time

After coming indoors, a dog peeing or pooping will stem from the atmosphere outside the house in certain instances. Too over-stimulating or disturbing for the dog might be the area allocated to go potty.

After all, how many times did it happen to you that you were outside the business or that you had an overwhelming desire to go only after you inserted the keys and turned the doorknob? Dogs may be comparable.

Why Does This Happen?

When they are let out, dogs who do not get enough time outside can get distracted. They can't wait to sniff around and romp and get rid of pent-up energy after being confined in the house for most of the day.

They get overwhelmed to the point of forgetting that they need to go potty with all of this sensory stimulation and enthusiasm to stretch their legs. They only realize the urgency and have an accident right on the spot until they're back inside. This can be seen with puppies regularly.

How to Deal With It:

Before playing, make it a habit for your dog to potty first outside. When he's sent out to the potty, stop talking and engaging with your dog; let him focus on sniffing around. If you're playing with your dog in the yard, play after the potty is gone. If possible, when it's quiet, take your puppy or dog out. Wait until the neighbors are inside if your dog is annoyed by the neighbors.

If he goes potty, don't let your puppy back inside. Once he goes potty, compliment him calmly (make sure you don't disturb him), encourage him, and let him spend some time in the yard before going back inside, playing, and exploring.

Encourage the dog to go potty BEFORE making time for play.

2. Fear and Anxiety

He does not feel relaxed enough to do his business if your dog is afraid of something in the yard or something he sees during walks. There could be so many sounds, or maybe other dogs, and people make him feel on the verge of it. They will keep it in until they are relaxed again when dogs are not comfortable. When a dog is over the mark, the last thing he cares about is going potty, so he might be scared of his life.

Dogs living in yards surrounded by invisible fences, also known as electric fences, can often get so frightened of the shock, they're afraid of being outside near the perimeters, so they'll just stick to their face with a worried look at the porch area. They also refer to these dogs as "porch sitters."

Why Does This Happen?

Going potty puts a dog in a vulnerable position. First of all, it takes time, which can make a difference when every second counts. Usually, a dog who detects risk would want to be able to jump into action on both of his four legs.

On top of that, dogs who pee or poop leave behind signs of themselves, and if they feel threatened by anything, it will place them in a vulnerable position.

Fearful dogs tend to disappear as much as they can, being tiny and almost invisible, so they do not want to leave behind traces that may attract predators (their urine or feces). Of course, today, as it was in the past, no killer animals are hunting them down, but those instincts may still prevail.

How to deal with it:

If a nervous dog has been rescued recently, it might be worth it to teach him/her temporarily to use pads indoors before he/she has adjusted to the modifications and has more faith.

When things are quiet, take your dog outside, if possible (e.g., avoid going out when the trash truck is around). You will want to focus on desensitizing your dog to anything he fears with the help of a specialist.

You will want to take it down and invest in a real fence or walk your dog on a leash to a potty if you own an electric fence. The emotional damage can take some time to reverse. Be patient with high-value treats and use them.

3. Changes to their timetables

Dogs are habitual animals, and they can be used at certain times of the day to go potty, and they enjoy their routines. A few minutes after eating and drinking, playing, or napping, puppies appear to spontaneously go potty. In the morning, adult dogs appear to go first, in the middle of the day, early in the evening, and right before going to bed.

Why Does This Happen?

Right before an interview or an exam, have you ever felt the need to go to the bathroom? A sudden change in their lives can cause anxiety, which can lead to self-relief. Dogs are no different... except that they cannot speak. If your dog's routine changes abruptly, it can cause your dog to relieve itself as a reaction to fear.

At odd times, a shift of schedule can also indicate eating and drinking, which makes the bowel movement unpredictable. Without 24/7 access to the outdoors, when he gets the unpredictable urge to go, a dog has no choice but to pee.

How to deal with it:

At specified times of the day, feeding puppies and dogs and maintaining their routine translates to consistent "outings." This ensures that it is easier to predict when a puppy or dog may need to poop as he or she is being fed at particular times of the day.

You can also set scheduled "potty times." This means first thing in the morning, right after meals, and once before bed, to take your dog outside. Make it clear to your dog that, before playing, he should do his business first. Keep this timeline consistent, and you will hopefully see a change instantly.

4. A Poor Diet

Feeding cheap foods from your supermarket will create bowel movements that are more regular and bulkier. Thus, even though it is more costly, quality dog food is better because more nutrients are consumed, and there is less waste as a result. It implies smaller stools and on a less-frequent basis.

Sudden changes in diet can also cause an upset stomach and a sense of urgency, especially if you have shifted from lots of fillers and grains to a lower-grade food.

What to Feed Your Dog:

Dogs like to eat real food, and if you have the time to make homemade food, try making vet-approved, simple, nutritious homemade dog food recipes.

When feeding kibbles, by reading the labels, make sure to educate yourself about how to pick high-quality dog foods. Go for natural, organic brands wherever possible, as a rule of thumb. There are fillers, meat or fish by-products, animal fat, liver meal, BHA, BHT, and other contaminants and additives in most commercial brands.

Only stay away from them!

5. Not Cleaning Up Accidents Thoroughly

Dogs have an instinct to relieve themselves where they have done it before, so he can remember the area as an acceptable potty area if your dog can smell his urine/poop, and will relieve himself there again.

How to cover up the scent of dog pee or diarrhea for good

With distilled white vinegar, spray the soiled region.

Wear latex gloves if the area is carpeted, and work the vinegar deep into the carpet fibers.

With a paper towel, wipe up the remaining liquid.

Sprinkle the surface with a generous amount of baking soda, ensuring that the whole area is coated. Again, work the baking soda into the carpet fibers with your fingertips if the area is carpeted.

Let the baking soda sit for a minimum of 1 hour.

To eradicate all traces of baking soda, vacuum the place.

If needed, follow up with a commercial dog stain and

odor cleaner.

Nature's Miracle, on the other hand, is a wonderful substance known for removing traces of odors because of its enzymes.

6. Substrate Preference

This is a little-known fact, but when they are 8.5 weeks old, puppies appear to form a substrate preference. This essentially suggests that puppies develop a preference for a surface to be used as their potty and become so used to a certain surface area that it is difficult for them to remove new surfaces.

Why Does This Happen?

So if a puppy has been trained to pee indoors on paper and then is taken into a new home where the puppy is required to pee outdoors on grass, the puppy may search for surfaces other than grass. This suggests that once outside, the puppy can keep it and then use the carpet once back inside.

For elderly dogs, the same goes. It will take some time for her to get used to using soil or grass during the potty time if your dog is used to removing it in a kennel or somewhere enclosed.

How to treat it

It's a good idea to inquire specifically what surface was used to let the puppy go potty when adopting a puppy from a pet shop, rescue, or breeder. If the puppy has been taught to use pads or newspaper, by putting a piece of newspaper or pad outside, you can eventually move the puppy to grass and allow the puppy to use it. You can then remove the newspaper or pad gradually or decrease its size to make more grass available. Do this repeatedly until only on grass does the puppy learn to potty.

7. Suffers From Separation Anxiety

Some dogs do not do well when left alone, but most dogs do not do well for long periods when left alone (4 hours or more). If you come home from work and discover messes in the home, consider your dog a separation anxiety candidate. Record the actions of your dog when he is left alone to confirm your argument. Whining, pacing, barking, howling, panting, digging, and pooping include signs of anxiety and pain.

Why Does This Happen?

Dogs are social animals. They may feel lost when they are left alone and don't understand the reason why. This induces nervousness, contributing to defecation or urination. Some dogs may even suffer from coprophagia, which is when they eat their excrement to conceal evidence. Poor breath and potential traces of feces left on the floor are clear signs of this

How to treat it

For more than half a day, try not to leave your dog alone. Have a neighbor, family member, or friend come during the day to feed and walk the dog if it can't be helped. You may also use a service like Wag Walking, where you pay someone to take your dog for a walk to visit your house during the day.

Ensure that when you are at home with your dog, you give her plenty of exercises and mental stimulation in the form of games and outdoor play. You may also try to leave a yummy bone for your dog to chew or hide treats around the house so that she has something to occupy her when you are gone. Check out these additional ideas to support dogs with separation anxiety.

8. Dog Is Too Old

A disorder is known as 'canine cognitive dysfunction," the dog equivalent of Alzheimer's disease, is developed by certain dogs as they age. In some activities, affected dogs can have a hard time, and potty training is one. Your dog may forget to go outside or send you signs that he has to go.

Some dogs may not be able to keep it together but may not have cognitive dysfunction.

How to deal with it

Limit just a few areas of the house to your dog. That would be preferable if you could restrict her to an uncarpeted place.

Cover with pads the places where your dog has access.

Don't beat your dog or scream at it. She couldn't help that. You're going to need patience and offering her encouragement. At this point in her life, clean-ups are a must, and you shouldn't expect her to do better.

If it's a serious issue, use doggy diapers, but ask your vet before buying the diapers. Some dogs can find it so unpleasant that they keep it in when they have to go, which is detrimental to their health.

Were you aware?

According to one study, 60 percent of dogs between the ages of 11 and 16 show certain cognitive dysfunction symptoms.

9. Recent Changes, New Pets, or New Family Members

Anything stressful introduced to the atmosphere of a dog will cause a decline in house training. It is not uncommon for a well-trained dog to have an accident in a new home shortly after moving. When a new dog is introduced to a house or if there are visitors or a new infant, a dog may also be upset.

Why Does This Happen?

The anxiety the dog experiences can only intensify by scolding the dog for these injuries. Setting a schedule after something different is implemented is the easiest thing to do. Feed your dog every day at regular times and take him outside before or after each meal to potty. She'll get used to the routine eventually, and the crashes will disappear.

Be sure to give your dog time to adapt to changes, as well. Plug-ins for pheromones, Bach flowers, and other soothing aids may assist during transitions. You can find this article helpful if your dog hates going out to the potty when it rains:

Support, my dog's not going to potty when it rains

10. Being Inside for Too Long

This may be evident, but it is worth noting. It is not your dog's fault for soiling at home if you are at work all day and making it late. Dogs should not be left at home for too long, and you are better off hiring a pet sitter or a dog walker if this is your case, so that your dog is free to go outside as needed.

If your dog is well housetrained, he'll have tried to keep it as long as he could, but when you were gone for so long, he probably couldn't keep it any longer. He's the last one in such a situation to be blamed.

Never scold your well-trained, home-trained dog for home soiling.

Is Your Dog Pooping for Revenge?

Dogs don't accept that feces is yucky, and they don't

realize that people don't want to clean up after them. So a human idea is a concept of pooping out of retribution. The dogs are clean.

Instead of taking it personally, explore why it could be more relaxed for your dog to relax in the house. On a rainy/snowy day or during a thunderstorm, it's always as easy as not wanting to go outside.

11. Medical Conditions

Several conditions can cause bowel movements to increase. With daily stools, some intestinal disorders can cause a sense of urgency, making it difficult for your dog to keep it in. Intestinal worms are also a source of bowel movements being more regular and something that should be excluded. Both dog owners should get the stools of their dogs tested at least once a year for parasites.

Possible Medical Causes:

- Parasites

- Intestinal worms

- Pain squatting

- Bladder infection

- Pain lifting leg

- Kidney stones

- Kidney failure

- Cushing's syndrome

- Addison's disease

- Liver diseases

- Dietary allergies or reactions

CHAPTER 5
HOW TO AVOID THE BIGGEST PUPPY POTTY TRAINING PITFALLS

Even if you try to do all right when it comes to puppy potty training, slip-ups can happen. It may be because, following obsolete advice, or more, miscommunication. This is why we have put together a list of mistakes usually made by owners when a puppy is raised in a crate, so you know what to avoid and help your pup adapt to their new environment.

10 Errors in Puppy Potty Training to Avoid

• Missing preparation for crate

According to our puppy training services team, crate training is important because it helps keep your pup healthy and speeds up the potty training process. Be sure to get your dog an adequately sized crate.

Not Overseeing

Be sure to keep an eye on your puppy if you are a new

dog owner since it just takes a few seconds for them to use the washroom inside. Overseeing them also allows you to understand their behavior. Using a crate will assist if you are unable to concentrate on them continuously.

Not paying attention to the Cues

When they decide to go out for a potty break, puppies appear to behave differently. It could be stuff like sniffing around, distracted acting, trying to leave the room, squatting, and more. Learning to know the signs will help in the training process for the puppy potty.

Not celebrating them •

Be sure to give them a treat after they do their business in the right place, in addition to rewarding your dog verbally. This will encourage them to understand that it is not good behavior to potty inside the building.

Getting Unreasonable Standards

Getting a few clean days while the crate trains your dog does not necessarily mean that they have it all worked out. It can take months for them to understand anything, or even more. It helps to be careful, not to slack off on the fundamentals of potty training.

Hold Times Do Not Understand

It helps to note when potty training your puppy that it takes them time to improve bladder control. By translating their age into hours in months, you will decide your pup's keeping period. A two-month-old puppy may be able to hold its bladder for two hours, but when they are busy and playing, this changes. An active puppy can have to go out every 20 minutes, depending on its age.

Not properly washing Stains

If an accident happens, in addition to getting rid of the obvious stains, make sure to treat the odor. This will help avoid incidents in the future at the same venue. Make sure to use a healthy cleaner dependent on enzymes.

Not Use of a Potty Phrase

Using phrases such as 'hurry up' or 'go potty' will motivate them while potty training your puppy. To get on with their business, you should teach them a word and use it as a prompt for them.

Use Potty Pads •

While potty pads are great training aids for training a puppy's crate, they can prolong the potty training phase.

54

Alternatively, you can have a particular location where they can do their business.

Punishing Your Pup for Accidents

With the potty training process, blaming your puppy for accidents will not help. Doing so can threaten and confuse them physically and may make them afraid to come near you. To help them understand the fundamentals, you can use constructive strategies instead.

CHAPTER 6
THE SECRET BEHIND SUCCESSFUL POSITIVE REINFORCEMENT TRAINING

How to Train Your Dog Using Positive Reinforcement

Training your dog by using positive reinforcement means that you reward the behaviors you like and disregard the behaviors you don't like. To reward your dog's good conduct, you can use praise, life rewards (such as sports, hikes, or car rides), or treats. One successful strategy is clicker training, but without the clicker, it is possible to use rewards. It's good to consider the many advantages of training your dog with positive reinforcement to help you get started.

Get Everybody Active

Good reinforcement makes it possible for anyone in the family to help in training the puppy. It doesn't require you to talk in a powerful voice, use your strength, or place yourself or a family member at potential risk. All should get in on the act in the family!

For example, encouraging your child to use certain dog training techniques, such as leash corrections and forms of punishment, can be unsafe. You should give your kids a couple of dog treats with positive reinforcement and show them the commands you're using. Children will be able to train your dog the same way you do, under your guidance.

Establishing Communication

Positive reinforcement helps you to communicate with your dog. When the dog does the desired action, you decide what you want your dog to do and let it know by offering rewards. It's more likely to replicate such positive habits when you praise your dog for doing stuff right because dogs seek to please.

It's not always that straightforward about retribution. A good example is punishing a dog for injuries caused by housebreaking. You catch the dog urinating on your carpet in this situation and scold it or resort to the age-old trick of a rolled-up newspaper smacking it. You aim to tell the dog that removing it inside your home is not appropriate. Instead, while you're around, dogs also learn that it's not possible to eliminate. This is one of the reasons why you can find that when left alone, your dog has accidents, but you never seem to catch it in the act. There's certainly an issue with communication; anxiety is just not an appropriate way for a dog to properly understand things.

You may prevent this misunderstanding with positive reinforcement. In the case of house training, you want to teach your dog to eliminate yourself outside rather than at home. You will reward the action you like, going to the bathroom outside, rather than punishing your dog. In this scenario, you give it plenty of praise and treats or let it go for some playtime any time your dog eliminates outside.

If you're careful and persistent, as it relieves itself outside while nothing occurs when it goes inside, your dog will learn that good thing occur. In an attempt to reap the benefits, your dog will soon be eliminating the outside because you managed to interact clearly with your dog.

Using it for various behaviors

It is not effective for any dog to use training techniques like leash corrections or other punishment types. In reality, punishment can help to make a behavior problem worse in certain instances.

Aggressive dogs are a prime example because they also become even more aggressive in the face of retribution. Similarly, nervous dogs can not respond well to even the smallest penalty. When punishment is used as a training tool, a dog afraid of certain persons or circumstances can become even more fearful. However, using positive reinforcement to train aggressive and nervous dogs, clicker trainers have reported great success.

Offer Mental Stimulation

Boredom, such as digging and repetitive chewing, is a major factor in common behavior issues. A perfect way to help keep boredom at bay is preparation. By simply adding a few quick, supportive training sessions to his day, you can be shocked at how much energy your dog can burn off.

Keep It Fun

For you and your dog, positive reinforcement training can be enjoyable if you keep training sessions short and cheerful. When dogs learn that training contributes to many positive results, many continue to see training sessions as playtime. In the hopes of having rewards, your dog will soon give you positive habits, and you're sure to get a smile out of the dog's eagerness to learn.

Strengthen Your Bond

Their dogs are their mates, partners, for most people, and become part of the family. Positive training strategies of encouragement will help improve the connection you have with your dog. While other training methods can teach your dog how to act, positive reinforcement can help you direct your dog while retaining its confidence and improving your relationship.

Put yourself in the role of your dog. If your boss physically forced you to get a job completed, would you feel relaxed at work? Or, are you more likely to enjoy working with compliments and perks with someone who provides a supportive environment? You're going to be more likely to work harder for the boss who praises you. In the same way, if your dog is looking forward to being praised rather than anticipating punishment, it's far more likely to enjoy your company.

Problems and Behavior Proofing

Consistency and persistence are the secrets to positive reinforcement. Watching your dog disobey a command can be very upsetting, and you may be tempted to express your frustration or disappointment at times. Know that dogs read much better than they understand words in body language, so you need to project positivity and say it.

Take a deep breath when you get upset, note that it's just a dog, do its best, and relax. Start with a smile and excited eyes again on a happier note. Your dog will pick up on that and look forward to the next thing you have in store for it.

The benefits you give should be different and things that appeal to your dog. Give a very delectable and addictive treat reserved only for training when teaching a new command or working on major issue habits. You can turn to their daily treats as your dog gets better or offer their favorite toy as a reward. Give plenty of praise, always. Soon you won't have to reward them every time, and for a job well done, your love will be enough.

5 WAYS TO REWARD A DOG USING POSITIVE REINFORCEMENT

One of the best ways to train a dog is to use positive reinforcement. You give the dog a treat to encourage an action you want to practice using the positive reinforcement approach. If you ask your dog to sit down, for instance, and he does it, you give him a treat. You reward his good conduct with it.

It will help make reward-based training enjoyable and interesting for both you and your dog to know which rewards your dog finds motivating. There are some excellent ways to praise the good conduct of a dog.

Treats

When they think of positive reinforcement, food rewards are what most people see. Treatments are quick and simple to dispense, and they're a perfect way to quickly reward conduct. It's quick to make sure your dog gets a correction when he performs a specific action if you use clicker training. When you try to get a dog to replicate a certain action in fast succession, treats are great for training sessions.

The downside to using treats to reward a dog is that bringing treats around isn't always easy. If you're dealing with a dog with food allergies, a weight problem, or digestive problems, it can also be a problem.

Games

Games are another enjoyable way for your dog to be rewarded. When your dog does anything you like, you can start a game your dog likes. Games are used in positive reinforcement training in almost the same way as food. Ask your dog to do something, and you'll launch a game as soon as he does what you've asked for. Tug-of-war and fetch have some nice game options.

It's simple to slip a training session into a tug-of-war or fetch game, too. Take out a doll or ball with a tug. Before the game starts, ask your dog to lie down. Give him the toy as soon as he sits, and begin playing. Offer your dog the "leave it" command during the game. Ask him to lie down until he lets go. Give him the toy or throw the ball as soon as he lies down. This is a nice way of reinforcing the training of your dog.

Attention From You

Most dogs enjoy nothing more than for you to get some snuggle time, praise, and other kinds of care. When your dog is well trained, your undivided attention may be seen as a reward.

Waiting before your dog comes to you for some petting is one way you can do this. Instead of instantly lavishing him with praise, ask him first to work for it. You may ask him, for instance, to sit or lie down. Give him some snuggle time if he does as you request. Step away for a few seconds if he doesn't, and then return and give him the order again. Your dog will soon learn that he gets plenty of your affection from those activities.

The Outdoors Access

The majority of dogs love to be outdoors. Fresh smells, fascinating sights, and all sorts of stuff to discover are there. You can use this as part of the positive reinforcement training program if your dog enjoys the outdoors.

Housebreaking is a perfect way for this kind of incentive to be used. On a leash, take your dog or puppy outside to the spot where you want him to relieve himself. Enable him not to explore. Only stick to the same place. Take him back inside if he does not relieve himself and try again a little later. If he's relieved, thank him and take him to the neighborhood for a stroll, encouraging him to stop and sniff and explore as much as he wants. Soon, your dog will learn that only after relieving himself in the right position will he get to spend time outdoors.

Playtime With Other Dogs

Many dogs are fond of playing with other dogs. For good conduct, you can use access to other dogs as a reward. Take a ride to your nearest dog park, for example. Have your dog wait until he's allowed to get out of his car. To give him access to the other dogs, ask him to sit or wait again until you open the gate. If he doesn't comply, you can wait for him or return to the vehicle. As soon as your dog discovers that the only way he can get playtime with other dogs is to respond to your commands, he will start offering these behaviors.

CHAPTER 7
WORST DOG TRAINING MISTAKE

Are you teaching the dog in the best possible way? The fact that you are teaching your dog at all means that everything is right for you. Don't let it get in the way of small mishaps. You will be shocked to learn that some variables may slow down the development of your dog, although they may seem trivial.

Here are the most common errors during dog training that people make. Are you guilty of any of these errors about dog training?

Waiting Too Long to Start Training

Training should begin the moment your dog, regardless of his age, comes home with you. Don't wait until he gets older and bad habits to grow. Dog training is not the same as handling behavior. The aim is to shape your dog's dog training actions and teach your dog how to react to specific phrases.

Young puppies may not be ready to learn advanced behavior, but you can start focusing on simple commands and house training. You'll forge a stronger relationship with your dog over time. He is going to mature and develop accustomed to the training sessions routine. You will then try interesting things like dog tricks and specialized training, such as animal-assisted therapy or agility.

Not Training Enough

Education is not something that you do once, and you're done. If you consistently train your dog, you can get the best results even after learning action or cue. Choose one thing to focus on at a time and at least two to three times a week to conduct short, productive training sessions. Find fun new stuff to teach your dog, but revisit the old fundamentals sometimes.

Your dog has never fully completed his training. Ideally, the dog will still be disciplined, even as he grows older. Ongoing training will help keep the abilities of your dog sharp. Training sessions with your dog are also enjoyable and a perfect way for the two of you to bond.

Taking a "One-Size-Fits-All" Approach

Don't just read one dog training book and conclude

that that's what you need to know. The same applies to talking to a friend you've got who knows dogs. There are several successful forms and systems of dog training out there, but no two dogs are exactly alike. Often, to create your training program, you need to take guidance from many sources and use all the details.

For your puppy, try out a few different things to see what works. To customize a plan that suits you and your dog, combine various training types. You may also want to pursue a few different classes of preparation. Don't give up too soon, but if anything doesn't work, don't be afraid to change things either.

Non-consistency

Consistent reactions are important for dog training at every level. You confuse your dog when you are incoherent in class. You can even find yourself promoting undesired habits unintentionally.

Let's say you make a rule that on the sofa, your dog is not allowed. Soon, you find yourself making the odd exception and letting him up there for one reason or another. If you turn around and get upset at him for being on the sofa, he's not going to understand why one moment is allowed, not the next.

Begging is another illustration of this flaw. If your dog never gets food from people who consume it, the habit of begging will not grow. At first, he could try it a few times, but continuously ignoring your dog or saying, "go to your place" would deter begging. If anyone gives him a bit of food, however, he'll equate begging with a reward, and in the future, he'll keep begging.

Rewarding the dog when he "sort of" does something is another sign of inconsistency. You praise him when his entire body is on the ground while teaching your dog to lie down. In the future, if you award him a "lie down" reward BEFORE his whole body is on the field, you are inconsistent. He can become confused and send you the incomplete version again the next time you say "lie down,"

Impatience

It takes time for dog training, and each dog learns at a different speed. As your dog is not catching on to something, try not to get stressed out or irritated. This would only make it worse because your dog is likely to get upset or stressed out.

Consider whether this is a good time to train if your dog cannot learn anything. Did the session go for too long? Remember to keep dog training sessions short and finish on a good note (about 10 to 15 minutes). Or, you can try to break down the behavior into smaller components and independently train each one. For this very reason, the action/cue "rollover" is also trained in phases.

Check the time next time you find yourself feeling restless. If it's been long enough (or if your dog appears irritated or disinterested), just wrap things up with a quick action that you know your dog can finish. Even if it means returning to the sitting cue, make sure to finish on a positive note. You will try to split up the training into smaller pieces later.

Another impatience is here: you ask your dog to sit down, and he doesn't. So, you keep saying the word "sit," and after 3 to 5 times saying sit, he eventually sits. You reward him, then, with a treat. You're just teaching him that the order was just a suggestion, and he should wait to sit down five times before you say it. Alternatively, repeatedly tell the command once and wait for the outcome. If your dog fails to comply with the first one, wait a few seconds, and start from the beginning (getting his attention first).

Tough Discipline

The majority of modern dog trainers believe that it is not very beneficial to use dog training discipline. In general, dogs are more likely to perform positive dog training for rewards. In certain cases, the use of mild aversives (like a spray bottle or a penny can) can be beneficial and do not appear to cause damage. Other items can, however, create a dangerous situation. Actions such as screaming, punching, alpha rolls, looking down, gripping the collar's scruff, and leash jerking include extreme discipline. Such behavior may have repercussions.

They can provoke your dog's angry reaction, putting you or other people in danger.

They could cause your dog to become frightened.

They can cause your dog to experience physical harm.

If you think it is important to have harsh discipline so that you can "assert dominance" over your dog, then you are all wrong about this. Humans' definition as a "pack leader" is obsolete and derives from outdated studies on dogs and wolves. Take the time to do your homework and learn to gain the love of your dog. A fun way to interact with your dog, not a teasing session, should be the training process.

Getting the Timing Wrong

When you reassure him that he will understand, your dog won't know that he has done anything good. Here's where positive pacing and reinforcement come in. Many trainers recommend using a clicker or a short word (like "yes"). Then, follow up with a reward instantly to make sure it's consistent with the clicker or phrase. Make sure that all of this happens soon (within a second or two). Your dog could equate the award with another action if the reward arrives a few seconds too late. When you are trying to get your dog to link behaviors to cue words, positive reinforcement is extremely important during early training.

When it comes to changing the dog's undesired habits,

the same thing goes. If you want to use aversives (which should be mild and held to a minimum or entirely avoided), make sure you immediately implement the aversive as the action occurs. If your dog is peeing in the house and you're not going to catch him until he's done, so you can't do anything. Any penalty would be correlated with something else after the fact (NOT the action of peeing in the house). When you pee on the floor, your dog will learn to be afraid, but he's not going to learn not to commit the action unless you catch him in the act.

Reinforcing the Wrong Behavior

Reinforcing undesired habits unintentionally is one of the most common errors made in dog training. You may not even consider it to be satisfying or reinforcement. Examples include soothing your dog when he's afraid, making him instantly bark in the house, or even giving him a stern talk-to when he's misbehaving.

Our dogs are beings who are social and seek our affection. Giving some kind of attention will tell your dog that his current conduct is good and should continue. And negative affection is better than none at all for many dogs. The only thing you can do if your dog does anything undesirable, such as jumping up on you, crying, or begging, is to withhold treatment until the auction ends.

Note: Avoiding the dog is not the best option if the undesired activity is self-rewarding, such as chewing furniture or jumping into the garbage. Instead, guide your dog's attention to a healthy activity that rewards, such as playing with a toy or going through exercise training.

Calling your dog to you for something disagreeable

If you knew you were going to get in trouble, be screamed at, or have any other bad stuff happen, would you want to go to a person? You wouldn't, of course, and your dog wouldn't either. You are effectively punishing him for coming back to you every time you call your dog to do something unpleasant. Eventually, when called, it'll stop your dog from coming. One of the most significant things you can teach your dog is to have a good recall. Don't ruin it with an error like this.

If you have something that your dog doesn't like (like a bath or a nail trim) to do, just go and get it instead of calling it. Try to calm down before giving your dog some kind of command/cue if you are upset about something.

After the inappropriate conduct has already happened, note that your dog can benefit little by being disciplined or screamed at.

Failing to Proof Behaviors

Proofing a behavior involves putting it into effect with various distractions in different environments. Too many people forget about this crucial aspect of the method of dog training. Once your dog has learned to sit in your living room, all he knows is that sitting means "put my bottom on the ground in the living room." The word sit could mean little or nothing to him when you are in the yard or the park and other dogs are around. Some dogs are better than others at generalizing. The majority very simply take lessons.

Start in a calm, controlled environment when you begin training an action. Then, switch with each session to various locations, progressively increasing the number of distractions. This can help fine-tune the responses of

your dog to your cues.

CHAPTER 8
THE TOP 5 GOLDEN RULES OF
DOG TRAINING

New Years' famously yield new resolutions, but are you aware that the start of January also marks the beginning of Your Dog Month's National Train? What could be a more appropriate way of enjoying this serendipitous rivalry than by working with your dog for a stronger training partnership?

To help make training with your dog safer and simpler, here are five golden rules while avoiding some of the most common mistakes that owners make.

Golden Rule #5: Resist repeating yourself

I can't tell you how many times I've seen someone call the name of a dog over and over again, getting louder with every repetition, while the dog appears to be ignoring anything around it or concentrating on something else intently. This approach annoys humans, who are always amazed when I call their dog's name and receive an answer on my first attempt.

Repeating a signal is perhaps the single greatest mistake seen by trainers when teaching new or seasoned owners how to work with their dogs. As people, it is in our nature to repeat ourselves to ensure that we are heard when we request others, and they are not honored. Sadly, in dog school, this is detrimental to our cause.

Dogs learn through association, and our task is to assist them in associating actions with certain words or movements. Recalling this, let's go back to our initial situation.

In an attempt to get her attention, the trainer (let's call him James) calls his dog's name (let's call her Sarah) five times. What are the practicable findings here?

If Sarah turns to look at James five times after hearing her name, either of them can get:

1. Rewarded for responding.

2. Punished for not responding sooner.

3. Ignored by James.

4. Sarah never acknowledges James.

In result 1, Sarah discovers that when she hears her

name, the right thing to do is wait for it to be called four more times because that's when the reward comes. She finds in Result 2 that reacting to her name results in retribution, something she will want to prevent in the future, making her even less likely to react to her name. In result 3, she discovers that her name is meaningless because nothing significant was produced; in other words, her name is white noise.

Rewarding outcome four does not give James any gain, and as outcome 2 tells us, punishing Sarah for non-compliance would only teach her in the future to escape punishment. That means that outcome 4 provides Sarah with the same learning outcome as outcome 3: her name is an insignificant white noise.

To maximize the rate of learning, trainers realize that we have to set dogs up for success. Scientifically, rewarding good conduct has been shown to achieve this, thus cultivating a human-canine relationship focused on mutual trust and affection rather than the urge to escape fear, pain, or retribution.

That's why I never ask a dog to carry out an action that I think is unlikely to happen, which leads me to...

Golden Rule #4: Promote foreseeable results

In other words, a game of odds.

Professional trainers recognize the value of setting dogs up for success and never ask for an action that is not likely to happen. It is important to note that training is rooted in science, and it is a method that relies on trial and error to identify us with solutions to the problem at hand, like all science.

When I watch an owner constantly call their dog's name, I look very closely at all aspects of the dog's environment to tell me why the dog does not respond.

Is this the dog's new location? Are distractions present there? Is the dog looking at something intently? Is sniffing the ground busy? To demonstrate a distant sound that the owner and I can not detect, are their ears twitching? What's with the owner? Does their tone of voice frighten the dog? In a confusing or potentially frightening way, are they gesturing?

I consider all of these small details when it's my turn to see if I can get an answer and wait until I think the dog is likely to comply with my order. Only then do I try to call the dog's name. Sometimes, this means waiting a few seconds until the dog has had an opportunity to process what is currently holding its attention.

Play the odds to maximize the chance of success and take your best guess. Remember the old Thomas Edison adage if you ever don't get desirable results:

I didn't struggle. I discovered 10,000 ways not to make a lightbulb.

James should have simply minimized his losses in our example above and avoided calling Sarah's name after failing to respond. Chances are, in her setting, she was simply focusing on something else, and she would have been able to respond to James if he had only waited a few seconds longer.

Golden Rule #3: Pay the sticker price

There is a price tag on any action.

At its heart, dog training relies on behavioral economics or the price we pay dogs to perform those acts. For basic actions like "sit," praise for dogs is also an acceptable paycheck. "But more challenging activities such as "stay" often require a greater incentive than a simple "Nice job!"

We, as people, continually navigate the social constructs of life. For instance, if I'm moving to a new house and want to borrow a truck from my friend, I need to make it worthwhile for him. It's also important to note that while a slice of pizza will be enough to thank me in this case, a friend who doesn't like Italian food is probably going to choose something else.

For dogs, the same is true. There is a price for any behavior, but the price for a single behavior can vary from dog-to-dog. Let me have an example for you.

I have two rescue dogs of opposite polar dispositions. Sonny, the most social creature I've ever met, is my basset hound. It can be a monumental challenge to try to get him to walk away from the chance to play with another human or dog. A slice of kibble has less meaning for him while we are at the dog park than the chance to play with another dog. But such as Plato salmon strips, a super high value treat? That's going to do the trick.

Now, Franky, my other guy, is a rehabilitated reactive dog. He can be very timid about new experiences, people, and other dogs in particular. Although we will never know for certain, we believe that he may have been neglected or used in combat circles before we adopted him. Franky could not care less about playing with other dogs now, unlike Sonny. So when I call him away from one of them, verbal encouragement is enough.

This is not to suggest Franky doesn't like to play. Instead, he only likes to play alone. I am confident that Franky will sell his soul for a chance to chase a tennis ball, given the opportunity. That's about the highest reward I can give him for value. Well, that and somebody dropped a burrito on the ground. But when I realize that we have a challenging training challenge ahead of us, I use it to my advantage. If my order is complied with by Franky, he gets to play fetch.

The more complex an application is, the bigger the paycheck. It's behavioral economics, and dogs have very little wiggle room on their sticker price in general. Note, what is satisfying is determined by the learner, not by the teacher.

Golden Rule #2: No pace for punishment

In school, we just discovered that the dog decides the importance of a reward, not us. The opposite of this is valid, as well. The learner (dog) also decides what is being punished. While we might find shouting as humans to run mill activity, a dog may find it aversive. This is why, as teachers, we should never ignore the possible implications of our actions.

Let's look at an example.

Sarah is a really big puller, and it's hard for James to walk her. To teach her to walk on a loose leash, he chooses to purchase a prong collar. Although James can see immediate relief from Sarah's leash pulling when using a prong collar, James can't see the issue with this aversive method.

Prong collars operate by inducing distress to teach a dog to stop experiencing pain while there is stress on the leash. Dogs feel 155 times more pressure from prongs on a very fragile area of their body when the same force is applied to both a prong and a flat collar.

In dog training, the inclusion of something negative to deter a behavior from happening is known as constructive reinforcement. Since dogs learn through association, other dogs, kids, strangers, bicycles, you name it, anything present in the dog's environment when feeling pain will take on a negative association. If this occurs, it is possible to shift the dog's desire to escape the discomfort around its neck to a desire to avoid items in its world. As the dog seeks to keep them from causing harm, this may lead to violence against other objects.

Studies has shown time and time again that it is more compassionate and profitable to reward good conduct than to punish bad behavior.

It is because of this that the ideal teaching tool for new, cruelty-free trainers is positive reinforcement. It has been scientifically demonstrated that reward-based training enhances the rate of learning, allows dogs to work harder for rewards, reduces the need for strong or aversive training tools, and facilitates a human-canine relationship based on confidence and respect rather than on the need for a dog to escape fear, pain or punishment.

It is also up to us to note that training must be performed at the dog's speed and minimize the use of constructive punishment in training. In a training situation, if we drive our four-legged friends too hard too soon, we can unwittingly cause them to develop painful emotional responses. And as we discovered with prong collars, violence also follows when this happens.

Consider this example.

Since Lucy doesn't know how to swim, the fear of being in hot, open water has grown. Before she first developed her faith in shallow waters, an ethical swimming teacher would not teach Lucy how to swim by throwing her into the deep end of a pool.

The same term applies to dog training, as well. If your dog is terrified of motorcycles, a recipe for failure is to ask it to sit quietly as many of them zoom past from a few feet away. Instead, in gradual measures, you need to work up to this sort of exposure. If you fail to understand and respect the fear of your dog, the next time it sees a bicycle coming its way, it is likely to respond aggressively to prevent the fear from occurring.

Golden Rule #1: Allow the dog to choose

"For behavioral health, the power to control one's outcomes is essential, and the degree to which a behavior reduction procedure preserves learner control is essential for developing a standard of humane, efficient practice."

Remembering that all action is conditional is important. This means that we need to alter the circumstances that cause it to happen to teach or adjust some behavior.

This may be a trainer's most critical piece of advice, which is somewhat ironic since this is possibly the most challenging golden rule to follow for owners.

Dogs are the learners during school, and we are the instructors. In other words, the learning conditions are regulated by humans. This suggests that the duty to teach or change a behavior does not belong to the dog. Rather, we must alter the circumstances that permit it to occur.

Let's say James comes home and sees Sarah on the sofa, where she's not supposed to be. James resorts to moving Sarah off the sofa after cueing Sarah to get down to no avail.

While on the surface, the way James solved this issue may seem harmless, he is venturing down a potentially dangerous path. Dogs have a strong instinct to preserve important resources such as food, toys, and places such as sleeping areas, as descendants of wild animals. This is referred to as resource guarding in dog training.

The loss of valuable resources to a wild animal can lead to death. Not only is James removing her right to choose where to sleep by driving Sarah off the couch, but he is also leaving the underlying emotional justification for sleeping on the couch unaddressed. That spot on the couch didn't lose its worth just because James pushed Sarah off, and if she values that resource enough, before his next attempt to remove her, she could preemptively growl or even bite James.

So, in this case, what could James have done differently? How was he able to teach Sarah to choose to leave the couch?

Empowering dogs to make decisions in their world makes it possible for them to control it, which creates ease, trust, and calm conduct.

James solved this issue by telling Sarah what she was doing wrong. But he would have been best served to teach her what the right thing is to do rather than sleeping on the sofa to retain her choice and power as a learner.

James needs to consider Golden Rule #3 to do this: pay the price of the sticker. The incentive for getting off the couch in the first place must be greater than the reward of being on it. James should lure her off with a high-value toy, treat, and to a suitable sleeping position the next time Sarah is caught on the couch. This way, Sarah considers the alternative more satisfying than sitting on the sofa, and she would prefer to stay off it in the future with some repetition.

CONCLUSION

By collaborating with them regularly, you will help your dog improve their bad habits. For your dog to make the shift you would like to see; consistency is the key. Stick to your rules and not encourage someone else to deviate from what you have taught when they contact the dog.

Your dog will start to get used to them once the techniques and training are etched in stone and will finally eliminate the bad behaviors. For a dog that does not want to obey your orders and refuses to comply, you may have a hard time.

When your dog is at peace and is obeying your orders, you will be less nervous. They must do that. To get them out and encourage them to be involved, you can feel relaxed.

Dogs are like infants, and you have to continue to nurture them and give them love and care. At the same time, to be a good member of your family, they must understand that they must accept correction.

9 781801 856393